I0161964

Summer's Delight

Majestic Reflection
Devotional Study Series
Book Three

A quarterly devotional by:

J. K. Sanchez

Summer's Delight: Book 3 of Majestic Reflection Devotional Study Series.
ISBN -13: 978-0692420676
ISBN – 10: 0692420673
Copyright © 2015 by J. K. Sanchez.
Published by: Button Lane Books Spanaway, WA 98387
Contact: Judy@jksanchez.com - www.jksanchez.com

Cover Photography by:
Majestic Reflection-J.K.Sanchez Photography
Cover Design by:
Turtleshell Press www.turtleshellpress.com

Dedication

To those who have begun and continue to walk on this narrow path of stepping into a life journey of pursuing the presence of our Lord Jesus Christ above all other life distractions. Enjoy the journey as you DELIGHT yourself in the Lord!

Contents

Acknowledgments

First and foremost, I am thankful for the support and consistent overflow of love from my husband, Dennis, my children, their spouses and my grandchildren. Each one of you is a DELIGHT that the Lord has blessed me with. My overwhelming Joy is found in each of your faces.

My continued love and appreciation to my sister, my friend, my almost TWIN in every way and <u>my editor</u>. Thank you Donna for always being there and knowing my thoughts before I speak them. Without you there would have been MANY mistakes.

We are blessed with many friends in our lives that are examples of Christ's many gifts. One such friend that has always walked a life filled with contentment and Delight in the Lord is my long time friend Patty. Thank you, my friend for an exemplary example of walking a life filled with contentment and Delight in Jesus.

And finally – but above all – my thanks to Jesus Christ who directed, inspired, and taught me (step by step) that to DELIGHT in Him brings me everything my heart desires. His presence and promise of favor and abundance are always there for me.

My life is not my own but a gift freely given back to the one who gave His life for me.

Introduction

My passionate journey for the presence of the Lord began within me decades ago and has drawn me to a narrow path filled with promise and freedom that I have never experienced before. During this journey I have found a deep <u>knowing</u> of my true identity as a daughter of the King and His amazing love for ME. As my path has narrowed to a place of the <u>one thing</u> – His face and presence - I have learned a new depth of love, rest, contentment and delight. These have shown me the importance of simplification that has brought me true freedom in Christ, as He has become Lord of my life.

His gift on the cross is just that – a gift. All of the "I can do's" are learning to lie down as my life is becoming focused on Him and what has already been "done" for me.

This book series has been ignited directly from that love and I desire to share, direct and encourage you to a place to meet Him, love Him, hear Him, see Him and be a lover of His presence as I am.

Most devotionals are 365 days of amazing deep thoughts that honestly, most of us don't make through. We miss a few days and give it up.

This devotional study series is:
     Based on a **quarter** and a 6-day week; (leaving day 7 for you to experience the filling of His presence as you gather with others).
     It is **perpetual** so it can be used year after year as you walk out this journey.
     It is **interactive** – it gives you a comparatively thought filled piece of writing and then builds with scripture and questions that will stir you to look deep within yourself - making this a personal growth experience.

     My desire is to direct you to His feet and see His transformation materialize in your life.

ENJOY THIS AMAZING JOURNEY OF DELIGHTING YOURSELF IN THE LORD!

The Beauty of a Bleeding Heart

There is a strikingly beautiful plant hidden in many gardens that intrigues me. The comparison of its name – "Bleeding Heart" to its visual grace appears to be an oxymoron.

She is stirred to awaken as soon as warming temperatures arrive. Quietly with no great fanfare her arrival begins as thin green shoots of soft foliage begin to emerge. Then with incredible grace an arching spray of dainty dripping heart shaped flowers cascade out of the center of the soft green mound. Appearing almost over night. Each of these tiny flowers resemble a perfect heart with a tiny drop of color coming from the tip, thus acquiring the name "bleeding heart".

Comparing this plant to your spiritual life is two fold, your heart and the heart of Christ.

The thought of a "bleeding heart" is one of pain. Hearts are broken, hurt and desensitized by hurts inflicted by others, by natural circumstances and by wrong decisions. However, the poured out life of Jesus shows a different kind of "bleeding heart".

His love for you was so great. He exchanged his life for yours. This exchange gives you eternal life and a new heart. His heart was a "bleeding heart" of grace and mercy as His blood was poured out just for you.

When you can take your "bleeding heart" and through the cross of Christ give that pain to him, receiving his forgiveness - then your heart is open to finding His love and acceptance.

The once "bleeding heart" in you is changed and becomes a thing of beauty. Your heart then is allowed to become just like the graceful beauty of the "bleeding heart" plant in my garden – free to be the beauty that is hidden within.

Let your "bleeding heart" be changed by giving it to Jesus. His love changes it into a transformed creation. Your choice is to accept His gift and allow the process to begin.

Day 1

Spend some time contemplating what *"The Beauty of a Bleeding Heart"* means to you.

1. What does this mean to you?

2. How does it apply to your life?

Journaling – writing down your thoughts, frustrations, God conversations, questions, desires, dreams and beyond is an important discipline to all areas of growth in our lives. This devotional will encourage that thought process. So write, write and write. Get a separate journal notebook and be prolific in your thoughts. Amazing things jump from the Holy Spirit out on to the page as we express ourselves.

Day 2

Jesus' "bleeding heart" of unconditional poured-out love for us was shown as he chose to give His life away to free us from our sins – all of them – past, present and future.

John 3:16 - "For God so loved the world, that he gave his only Son, that whoever believes in him should not perish but have eternal life."

1. Have you said "good bye" to your past and laid it at the feet of Jesus? Take time with Jesus today to be free of the "baggage" from your past.

Whether you have just decided that it was time to lay your past down and accept His free gift* or you have known Christ for many years; contemplate that gift and the victory it has brought to your life.

2. What does His gift of salvation mean in your life today?

3. How do you see His continual love and forgiveness working in your life today?

*(Accepting Jesus is simply acknowledging your sin and need for forgiveness. Asking Him to forgive you and believing He died for you, that he forgives you, loves you and has the very best in store for you. It's that simple. Welcome to the Kingdom of God!)

Day 3

Psalm 34:18 - The Lord is near to the brokenhearted and saves the crushed in spirit.

Psalm 147:3 - He heals the brokenhearted and binds up their wounds.

A "bleeding heart" can be hard to rise above. We are often told to "just get over it"; "put your big girl panties on" or "pull yourself up by your boot straps" but reality doesn't work that way. However, we have been given a promise of healing through the cross of Christ. What man cannot do – He can.

1. Consider these scriptures in the light of your own brokenness. How can you apply them?

2. What hurts have you held onto that can be given over to His healing?

Day 4

Hebrews 4:16 - Let us then with confidence draw near to the throne of grace, that we may receive mercy and find grace to help in time of need.

Psalm 62:5-8 - For God alone, O my soul, wait in silence, for my hope is from him. He only is my rock and my salvation, my fortress; I shall not be shaken. On God rests my salvation and my glory; my mighty rock, my refuge is God. Trust in him at all times, O people; pour out your heart before him; God is a refuge for us. Selah

Knowing that we have a Father that calls us to come to him with everything that is hurting – every scraped up knee – allows us freedom to pour out our "bleeding heart" knowing that we are heard, loved and forgiven. He promises to those who trust in Him that He will be the strength and fortress of their lives.

1. Spend some time today going in confidence to the feet of Jesus. Lay down the past scraped up knees and move forward as a new creation.

Day 5

Ezekiel 36:26 - And I will give you a new heart, and a new spirit I will put within you. And I will remove the heart of stone from your flesh and give you a heart of flesh.

2 Corinthians 5:17 - Therefore, if anyone is in Christ, he is a new creation. The old has passed away; behold, the new has come.

Freedom from past hurts will allow the hidden beauty within you to begin to flourish. Decide today to rejoice in His freedom.

1. What does it mean to you to be " a new creation"?

2. How and in what ways is Christ changing your heart of stone into one of flesh?

Day 6

Re-read *"The Beauty of a Bleeding Heart"*.

1. What have you learned this week about walking in freedom from past hurts?

2. What are the keys for you to stay free?

Through Christ you Reign in Freedom!

No Weeds, No Fences in the Kingdom

I love to meander and enjoy a beautifully manicured flower garden – no fences, no weeds, no encroaching grass and no invasion of space by another species. Unfortunately those gardens don't exist in most neighborhoods unless there is a full time gardener employed.

Just as a well cared for garden allows for both beauty and fragrance to meld together for an unimaginable aroma - each of you are filled with treasures of different types – gifts that have been given to you. Your specific type and fragrance is different from the one next to you and it is only made better by their presence alongside.

When you walk in the Kingdom of God with your eyes focused on Christ - your individual aroma can be enjoyed and the very fragrance within permeates your atmosphere.

However, often you will find yourself trying to smell or look just like the one next to you or assume they are in your way and begin pushing them out. Your own needs for acceptance, validation and affirmation begin to change the look that your gardener had planned for this garden. Fences begin to divide up the landscape; weeds, encroaching grass and invasion of space change the garden from His intended plan.

Thankfully, you have a loving full time gardener who can adjust those unwanted weeds, encroaching grass and unnecessary invasion of space by lovingly showing you who you are in Him. Your significance and purpose can be trusted into His hands.

If your focus is always on Christ – He will quickly redirect any unwanted change to His landscape in your life.

With a full time gardener on your side your individual aroma can be enjoyed and the fragrance within will merge with those around you. You then begin to saturate your atmosphere with a scent of completeness that only comes from many single focused scents becoming one.

Your Christ focus will eliminate the encroaching grass and all weeds. There will be no need for fences for this garden will have no boundaries. Its beauty will be as astounding as your individual varieties. For now, as each of you with a singular scent produce exactly what and where the gardener planned. Honor for and encouragement of the species on your right and on your left only enhances this garden. For only when it melds into one is its true purpose seen.

Join me as you allow your scent to rejoice in a single Christ centered focus. Allow Him access to pull all weeds, all grass and pull down all fences.

Let's walk in a Kingdom side by side that has no weeds, no fences or self focused distractions.

11

Day 1

Spend some time contemplating what *"No Weeds, No Fences in the Kingdom"* means to you.

1. What does this mean to you?

2. How does it apply to your life?

Day 2

Ephesians 5:13-17 - But when anything is exposed by the light, it becomes visible, for anything that becomes visible is light. Therefore it says,
"Awake, O sleeper, and arise from the dead, and Christ will shine on you."

1 Thessalonians 5:23-24 - Now may the God of peace himself sanctify you completely, and may your whole spirit and soul and body be kept blameless at the coming of our Lord Jesus Christ. He who calls you is faithful; he will surely do it.

1. How do your needs for acceptance, validation and affirmation affect the garden you live in? This pertains to home life and church life.

2. Take time today to allow the Holy Spirit to shine light on areas where some weeding needs to be lovingly done and journal your thoughts.

<u>Day 3</u>

Micah 7:18-19 - Who is a God like you, pardoning iniquity and passing over transgression for the remnant of his inheritance? He does not retain his anger forever, because he delights in steadfast love. He will again have compassion on us; he will tread our iniquities underfoot. You will cast all our sins into the depths of the sea.

Romans 8:1 - There is therefore now no condemnation for those who are in Christ Jesus.

1. What areas of self-focused distraction do you see causing fences to be built around you?

2. Trusting in the "always available" forgiveness of Christ allows us to grow. Allow some time today to get rid of those fences and remember the two scriptures above are promises of His love and forgiveness.

14

Day 4

Romans 8:37 - No, in all these things we are more than conquerors through him who loved us.

II Corinthians 3:17 - Now the Lord is the Spirit, and where the Spirit of the Lord is, there is freedom.

1. How has laying down self-focus and readjusting to a Christ focus brought you freedom?

Spend some time today to "be still" before Him allowing a Christ focus to become a way of life.

<u>Day 5</u>

Isaiah 32:17 - And the effect of righteousness will be peace, and the result of righteousness, quietness and trust forever.

Ephesians 2:10 - For we are his workmanship, created in Christ Jesus for good works, which God prepared beforehand, that we should walk in them.

Matthew 13:44 - "The kingdom of heaven is like treasure hidden in a field, which a man found and covered up. Then in his joy he goes and sells all that he has and buys that field."

Seeing the need for and beauty of the individuals who have been placed around you is like finding hidden treasure in a field. There are buried treasures within each of them. Their amazing fragrances will meld with your own to create the atmosphere that brings freedom and opens the very gates of heaven on earth. Walking in freedom as one is what it means to have no weeds or fences – a kingdom without boundaries.

1. Take time today to think of those around you and write down several unearthed treasures you see in each of them?

2. How can you honor those people today, encouraging the hidden treasures?

3. Step out and apply one of the above.

Day 6

Re-read *"No Weeds, No Fences in the Kingdom"*.

> 1. How has your garden been tended to this week?

> 2. When weeds and fences are removed we encounter freedom. How did that affect you this week?

> 3. Journal any thoughts that the Holy Spirit stirred as you re-read this weeks prose.

You are Righteous in Christ!

Blooming In His Love

Great anticipation is stirred within me as I walk in my garden and watch the flower buds beginning to swell. Their individuality silently waiting to erupt into the hidden beauty they were created to be.

The understanding of the love of Christ within you is like the promise hidden within the budding flower – a transformation waits.

Waiting as the fullness of time passes - these buds will reveal an explosion of color, texture and scent as each one comes into its own fullness of beauty. This is shown off in a spectacular array as each specific flower exhibits its own created characteristic. Even when they are the same flower, side by side – they show off differences and individuality in their colors and shapes.

You too are similar in comparison. Your budding life in Christ comes into full bloom as you enter into the place of knowing the love and true identity that you carry as a child of the King. Only then can you come into full bloom and show forth the beauty of who you were created to be.

The process from bud to full bloom can't be rushed without damage or destruction to the flower.

Children love to pick a flower bud and then one petal at a time peel it apart. They are hoping to see the treasure that is hidden in the center.

Disappointment and frustration show on their little faces as they find only a hand-full of shriveling petals once the center is unveiled. They do not realize that the delight in its beauty is only found when time has completed its work.

So relax, rest in His presence, be content in the journey. Allow the truth of His love and acceptance to begin the process. As you "bloom in His love" the revelations of treasures hidden within you will soon burst into full bloom.

Day 1

Spend some time contemplating what _"Blooming In His Love"_ means to you.

1. What does this mean to you?

2. How does it apply to your life?

<u>Day 2</u>

1 John 4:16 - So we have come to know and to believe the love that God has for us. God is love, and whoever abides in love abides in God, and God abides in him.

1. What does it mean to abide?

2. Spend time today journaling your understanding of God's love for you.

Day 3

Romans 8:19 - For the creation waits with eager longing for the revealing of the sons of God.

II Corinthians 4:7 - But we have this treasure in jars of clay, to show that the surpassing power belongs to God and not to us.

The treasure hidden within each of us is like a budding flower – it can't be rushed into blooming. We must patiently wait for His timing. It is not for us to pull off the petals looking for what's inside. Learning to be content where we are is part of the blooming process.

1. What areas of your life do you feel are in the process of coming into full bloom?

2. Are you trying to "help" God in the growth process or are you able to be content in the waiting process?

3. Spend time today in His presence allowing contentment to wash away the "trying" and journal your thoughts

Don't fret if you find yourself in the "helping" God mode. We all struggle with that. Remember that we are the clay jar and He is the one who has full control of the growth process of our lives.

Day 4

1 John 3:1-2 - See what kind of love the Father has given to us, that we should be called children of God; and so we are. The reason why the world does not know us is that it did not know him. Beloved, we are God's children now, and what we will be has not yet appeared; but we know that when he appears we shall be like him, because we shall see him as he is.

Romans 8:16-17 - The Spirit himself bears witness with our spirit that we are children of God, and if children, then heirs—heirs of God and fellow heirs with Christ, provided we suffer with him in order that we may also be glorified with him.

1. What benefits belong to a son or daughter?

2. Do you see yourself as a Child of God? What does that mean to you?

Day 5

Isaiah 55:10-11 - "For as the rain and the snow come down from heaven and do not return there but water the earth, making it bring forth and sprout, giving seed to the sower and bread to the eater, so shall my word be that goes out from my mouth; it shall not return to me empty, but it shall accomplish that which I purpose, and shall succeed in the thing for which I sent it.

Jeremiah 29:11-13 - For I know the plans I have for you, declares the Lord, plans for welfare and not for evil, to give you a future and a hope. Then you will call upon me and come and pray to me, and I will hear you. You will seek me and find me, when you seek me with all your heart.

When we have confidence in the love of Christ and conduct our lives walking in the understanding of our true identity as a child of the King then we can confidently delight in who we are and who He has created us to be. This deep contentment brings freedom in every area. The Treasures within begin to bloom as His time comes to completion and we are content in His plans and purposes for our lives.

1. What areas of your life are you not walking in contentment in?

2. Refresh your thinking regarding Christ's love for you; who you are as a child of the King and trust Him with those areas. Journal your thoughts as you spend time at the feet of Jesus today.

Day 6

Re-read *"Blooming In His Love"*.

1. Summarize your thoughts about this weeks study?

2. What did the Holy Spirit reveal to you personally this week?

You are a Child of the King!

The Growth Process of a Seed

With excitement we prepare our gardens and plant seeds with anticipation of the end result. Consideration of the required process that the seed must take from beginning to end is not given much thought. However, let's consider that today.

We place each individual seed into the soil. Each one is given equal nutrition, water and sun. The seed does nothing. Slowly – over the appropriate time – it begins to germinate. Still – to our eyes - the seed is doing nothing, the process is just occurring. Then like an eruption from within – it sprouts new life that pushes up through the soil. But the seed did nothing but WAIT. The life and the harvest come from within at just the right time.

Now what if the gardener became impatient and came back every day, pulling back the soil to check if the seed had grown yet. Or he may think that extra water or more fertilizer will make it grow faster. However, these excesses will only cause death or unproductive seeds – the planned harvest within the seed is destroyed.

Patience – waiting – trusting in the pre-planned purpose of that seed is the gardeners' hardest chore.

Each seed has a harvest quota programmed into its DNA – some 30, some 60 and some 100 fold.

We behave like the anxious gardener when we actually are the seed.

We find ourselves running here and there for better and more teaching, or working harder to achieve a place in the Kingdom. These activities are like adding excess water or fertilizer to the seed and often it results in stunted or destroyed seed.

Our place – as the seed - is to rest and wait. Trusting that where we have been placed is a nutrient rich well-watered soil. It will bring forth that which is within as it is consistently shined upon with His warmth. Our Heavenly Father has a planned harvest that He has placed within each of us – 30, 60 or 100 fold. It is not up to the seed to make it happen. The DNA of whom and what we are to produce will be ignited and will erupt from within, bringing forth a fruitful harvest filled with completeness. No extra fertilizer required. Be patient and wait for the treasures placed within you to come forth.

As you focus on the face of Jesus – His love and rest will bring contentment to the destiny that is placed within you. His revelation and direction will be made clear. Freedom and refreshment will be your very heartbeat as your seed produces exactly what it is destined for.

Day 1

Spend some time contemplating what *"The Growth Process of a Seed"* means to you.

    1. What does this mean to you?

    2. How does it apply to your life?

Day 2

Titus 3:4-7 - But when the goodness and loving kindness of God our Savior appeared, he saved us, not because of works done by us in righteousness, but according to his own mercy, by the washing of regeneration and renewal of the Holy Spirit, whom he poured out on us richly through Jesus Christ our Savior, so that being justified by his grace we might become heirs according to the hope of eternal life.

Acts 1:7 - He said to them, "It is not for you to know times or seasons that the Father has fixed by his own authority.

1. Do you find yourself as the anxious gardener – looking for more teaching and more opportunities to prove yourself in the Kingdom? Or are you content to trust that the hidden treasures within you will begin the germination process in His timing?

2. Spend time with the Lord today considering the above answer and journal His directions and thoughts from that time.

Day 3

Psalm 37:7 - Be still before the LORD and wait patiently for him; fret not yourself over the one who prospers in his way, over the man who carries out evil devices!

2 Corinthians 9:10 - He who supplies seed to the sower and bread for food will supply and multiply your seed for sowing and increase the harvest of your righteousness.

Hebrews 11:1 - Now faith is the assurance of things hoped for, the conviction of things not seen.

Waiting on the Lord, laying down our own plans and busyness as well as trusting Christ with the details of our life is what faith is all about. The process of our faiths growth is much like the seed sown in soil. Without first hiding the seed in the soil, the proof – the eruption of a fruitful plant – will never occur.

Time at the feet of Jesus is essential to that growth process.

1. When and where do you find a place of
   stillness with the Lord?

2. How can you implement a time to wait
   on the Lord daily in that place?

Day 4

Psalm 1:3 - He is like a tree planted by streams of water that yields its fruit in its season, and its leaf does not wither. In all that he does, he prospers.

Take time today to sit in quiet - waiting in His presence. Drink in the peace of God. Lay all the daily distractions down and journal your thoughts about contentment with where you are in the growth process.

Day 5

Mark 4:8 - And other seeds fell into good soil and produced grain, growing up and increasing and yielding thirtyfold and sixtyfold and a hundredfold."

Proverbs 16:9 - The heart of man plans his way, but the Lord establishes his steps.

You were born with a specific DNA sequence that is unique to only you. You cannot change that - it is who you are. Similarly, what God planned for your life to produce – when your seed begins to flourish – will produce what it was intended to. You cannot work harder to make a seed that was meant to produce 30 fold produce 100 fold.

We have for many years been told to try harder, work smarter, and produce more. However, in the Kingdom He is the master gardener with the full manifest regarding who, what and when that seed will produce. It is time to wait patiently for His time – not ours.

1. What is your understanding of the Mark 4:8?

2. Have you been making your own plans and working hard or trusting in Christ to establish your steps?

3. Take time today at the feet of Jesus deciding which way is His plan for you. Journal your discovery.

Day 6

Re-read *"The Growth Process of a Seed".*

1. As you have focused this week on the face of Jesus, what revelations in your own life have you found about being fruitful in the Kingdom?

You are a Fruitful Seed!

Summers Stirring of Our Senses
The Gift of Sight

The fullness of summer expresses itself as it erupts around us. All five of our human senses are bombarded with the treasure-trove of experiences that come into the atmosphere as this extravagant season boldly fulfills its time.

We experience summer through sight, sound, taste, touch and smell as each sense is stirred within us.

We each find delight in summers abundance according to our own personal past and current circumstances. However, let's look at summer's expressions that we physically experience through our senses. Let's begin to compare our sensory experiences with the promises of Christ's contentment in our lives.

Through the visual gift of sight we experience the vivid explosion of color as flowers change places like colorful dancers on a dance floor.

Summer brings to our vision bluer skies, fluffier clouds and clearer star filled nights. Our sight is refreshed at the visual expression of cool waters as they splash over river rocks and crash as waves upon the warm sandy shores.

So many sights of peace come into our vision during summers outpouring of abundance and most of them bring deep warmth – a center of contentment - to us physically, emotionally, mentally and spiritually.

God revelations – communications - come through a sight process. That sight can be an actual vision but most likely it's sight awareness from within. That awareness brings refreshing and peace.

With a single focus on Christ you will become visually attuned to life transforming understanding – internal sight – of who He is, what He did for you at the cross, and His love for you.

His gifts of refreshing and peace come from a hand filled with abundant love for you His child.

Allowing His reign and rule in your life, trusting that He always "has your back" will bring contentment in your journey. Enjoy a summer filled with eyes only for the face of your beloved.

Day 1

Spend some time contemplating what *"Summers Stirring of Our Senses – The Gift of Sight"* means to you.

1. What does this mean to you?

2. How does it apply to your life?

Day 2

Psalm 119:18 - Open my eyes, that I may behold wondrous things out of your law.

Matthew 13:16 - But blessed are your eyes, for they see, and your ears, for they hear.

Spending time in the Bible opens our eyes to amazing promises and truths. Through the Holy Spirits direction we see things that can change our lives.

1. Take some time today to read the Bible. John and Acts are two great places to start or re-read. As you read today what did you see that spoke to where you are in your life today?

2. Journal your thoughts.

Day 3

Matthew 5:8 - "Blessed are the pure in heart, for they shall see God.

Psalm 121:1-2 - I lift up my eyes to the hills. From where does my help come? My help comes from the LORD, who made heaven and earth.

As we trust in the unconditional love of Christ our understanding of His Love grows. The internal awareness of God and His communication to us can be found daily if we open our hearts to listen.

1. Spend time journaling your own thoughts regarding revelations He has spoken to you today from these two scriptures.

Day 4

Psalm 13:5-6 - But I have trusted in your steadfast love; my heart shall rejoice in your salvation. I will sing to the LORD, because he has dealt bountifully with me.

1. Summer is a delight to every area of our senses. Look around and jot down 5 summer expressions that you see visually that speak of our loving Fathers hand in nature.

2. Rejoice in those today.

Day 5

Luke 11:33-36 - "No one after lighting a lamp puts it in a cellar or under a basket, but on a stand, so that those who enter may see the light. Your eye is the lamp of your body. When your eye is healthy, your whole body is full of light, but when it is bad, your body is full of darkness. Therefore be careful lest the light in you be darkness. If then your whole body is full of light, having no part dark, it will be wholly bright, as when a lamp with its rays gives you light."

Numbers 6:24-26 - The Lord bless you and keep you; the Lord make his face to shine upon you and be gracious to you; the Lord lift up his countenance upon you and give you peace.

1. The above scriptures speak of light within us, and the Lords face and peace upon us. When our eyes are focused on Christ – light reigns within us and then peace and contentment follow. Are there any areas where the light has faded in your life?

2. How can you stir up and re-light the flame in that area?

3. Time in His presence always will ignite - focus on the face of Jesus as you sit at His feet. Spend time in His presence today stirring. Journal your thoughts from that time.

Day 6

Re-read *"Summers Stirring of Our Senses – The Gift of Sight"*

1. What new revelation from God did you receive this week as you spent time in His presence?

2. Can you apply this directly to your daily life? If so - where?

HE is the Light!

Summers Stirring of Our Senses
The Gift of Sound

Our senses play a large part in how we experience things in our lives. Summer explodes with sounds that create lasting life memories. As spring moves into summer the sound of chirping birds and buzzing bees, as well as the scurry of rabbits and squirrels begins to stir anticipation of new life as summer explodes on the scene.

As we listen we hear the contagious joyous laughter of children, the clicking metallic sound of a sprinkler that delivers life-giving water to grass and seedlings, as well as the gurgle of streams and the crash of waves.

These sounds are only enjoyed if we listen and respond. If the busy activity of life overtakes our thoughts we can easily miss the enjoyment of these amazing gifts of summer.

Sound can come in thunderous explosions or in the slightest whisper. One is heard and felt – easily not missed. The other – is missed by most.

Tuning your spiritual ears to hear the very whisper of your Lord requires a deep place of contentment to rise within. This contentment comes as you willingly choose to listen.

As you surrender your busyness in exchange for His plans, step into a life that He directs and humbly consistently go to Him with a cry of "less of me and more of you" the listening process unfolds. These decisions will allow you to begin a journey of His destiny – one that will contentedly produce a courageous life full of faith.

Listening and responding in your spiritual life is often missed or lost because of distractions. Taking time to stop and listen to what the Holy Spirit speaks to you through the direction of Christ - requires a time where you stop and sit at the feet of Jesus.

Choose today the ONE THING that is important – to sit at the feet of your Lord. Then you will truly enjoy the gift of sound – hearing Him call your name!

Day 1

Spend some time contemplating what *"Summers Stirring of Our Senses – The Gift of Sound"* means to you.

    1. What does this mean to you?

    2. How does it apply to your life?

Day 2

Luke 10:38-42 - Now as they went on their way, Jesus entered a village. And a woman named Martha welcomed him into her house. And she had a sister called Mary, who sat at the Lord's feet and listened to his teaching. But Martha was distracted with much serving. And she went up to him and said, "Lord, do you not care that my sister has left me to serve alone? Tell her then to help me." But the Lord answered her, "Martha, Martha, you are anxious and troubled about many things, but one thing is necessary. Mary has chosen the good portion, which will not be taken away from her."

The daily distractions of life were part of both Martha and Mary's worlds but Mary made a choice to STOP and sit at the feet of Jesus – her Lord. Did all the serving get taken care of? Not like Martha felt was necessary. But Jesus thought differently. We need to tune our spiritual ears away from the busyness of life and listen to the whisper of the Holy Spirit.

1. In the above process, where do you find yourself today?

2. When your life feels like "Martha's" what choices can you make that will change it?

Take time to sit at the feet of Jesus today and just listen.

Day 3

Luke 8:14-15 - And as for what fell among the thorns, they are those who hear, but as they go on their way they are choked by the cares and riches and pleasures of life, and their fruit does not mature. As for that in the good soil, they are those who, hearing the word, hold it fast in an honest and good heart, and bear fruit with patience.

John 15:5 - I am the vine; you are the branches. Whoever abides in me and I in him, he it is that bears much fruit, for apart from me you can do nothing.

I Peter 5:7 – casting all your anxieties on him, because he cares for you.

Our faith is matured as we abide at the feet of Jesus. As we place our lives and all of the details in His hands and actively make Him our Lord our lives are transformed and radiate His freedom. If we allow the cares and distractions to take over - stress reigns and joy flees. His plan is for us to Delight in His presence and live a life filled to over flowing with joy and freedom.

1. In our daily life we find cares and worries "popping up" all around us. How we walk through them is a choice. Contemplate recent choices you have made – the stressful "gotta do it all my way" or the peaceful "stop, breath and sit awhile with Jesus way" what were the results of doing it each way?

2. How can you apply a lifestyle like "Mary" - Thus, resulting in lifestyle results of peace?

Day 4

Job 26:2-14 - "How you have helped him who has no power! How you have saved the arm that has no strength! How you have counseled him who has no wisdom, and plentifully declared sound knowledge! With whose help have you uttered words, and whose breath has come out from you? The dead tremble under the waters and their inhabitants. Sheol is naked before God, and Abaddon has no covering. He stretches out the north over the void and hangs the earth on nothing. He binds up the waters in his thick clouds, and the cloud is not split open under them. He covers the face of the full moon and spreads over it his cloud. He has inscribed a circle on the face of the waters at the boundary between light and darkness. The pillars of heaven tremble and are astounded at his rebuke. By his power he stilled the sea; by his understanding he shattered Rahab. By his wind the heavens were made fair; his hand pierced the fleeing serpent. **Behold, these are but the outskirts of his ways, and how small a whisper do we hear of him! But the thunder of his power who can understand?**

The might and power of God are indescribable. The above scripture shows a clear picture of how BIG He is but also shows His love and gentle ways. He whispers to us. Often we miss that beckoning call to come away and sit with Him.

1. Take time today to just listen. List both the loud and quite voices that you hear in nature?

2. Contemplate the vast power of our God and rejoice in that today.

Day 5

John 16:13 - When the Spirit of truth comes, he will guide you into all the truth, for he will not speak on his own authority, but whatever he hears he will speak, and he will declare to you the things that are to come.

I Corinthians 2:9 - But, as it is written, "What no eye has seen, nor ear heard, nor the heart of man imagined, what God has prepared for those who love him"

During the summer nights we often find ourselves sitting outdoors listening to the fire crackle or the crickets chirp. Stop and take time to listen for His whisper.

1. The whisper of the Holy Spirit guides and directs us daily if we listen. Take time today to stop, sit and listen.

2. Journal thoughts or directions that you heard today as you waited on the Lord.

Day 6

Re-read *"Summers Stirring of Our Senses – The Gift of Sound"*.

1. How has your faith been stirred and stretched to stop, sit and listen this week?

You are His Delight!

Summers Stirring of Our Senses
The Gift of Taste

When you think of summer's abundance how can you help but find your mouth salivating.

Our senses are stirred at the thought of juicy dripping watermelon, fresh corn on the cob covered with warm butter, a red ripe strawberry bursting with sweetness along with many other amazing flavors found only in summer.

Our sense of taste is another gift that correlates with the abundance of Christ's promises that have been provided to us.

To taste in the natural requires us to reach out and take something into us. It's a choice we have to make. Sight and sound occur around us; however taste is one of our choice senses.

In the spiritual, God has also given us the choice to taste and see His goodness.

To enjoy foods placed before us "to nibble" vs "digging in" are two completely different things.

When we nibble on something it is just a little bite, usually because we are not sure if we will like it or not. When we dig in with no hesitation it is because we know what is placed before us is filled with amazing goodness.

Spiritually we often nibble for many reasons – fear being the biggest. Jesus and the Holy Spirit both came to show the goodness of God, His love for you and His promise that He will never leave you. Fear of anything is not in the equation. His love for you BREAKS off all fear.

If you are a "nibbler" in the spiritual chose today to believe that what He has for you is a plate filled with amazing goodness. Join me as we "dig in" and enjoy all of what He has for us. Taste and see just how good He is.

<u>Day 1</u>

Spend some time contemplating what *"Summers Stirring of Our Senses – The Gift of Taste"* means to you.

1. What does this mean to you?

2. How does it apply to your life?

Day 2

1 John 4:18 - There is no fear in love, but perfect love casts out fear. For fear has to do with punishment, and whoever fears has not been perfected in love.

Deuteronomy 31:8 - It is the LORD who goes before you. He will be with you; he will not leave you or forsake you. Do not fear or be dismayed."

1. Are you a "Nibbler" or one who "digs in"?

2. Are there areas of fear that you walk in? If so how can you apply the above two scriptures in those areas to find freedom?

Day 3

Isaiah 26:3-4 -You keep him in perfect peace whose mind is stayed on you, because he trusts in you. Trust in the LORD forever, for the LORD GOD is an everlasting rock.

Psalm 9:10 - And those who know your name put their trust in you, for you, O LORD, have not forsaken those who seek you.

1 Peter 2:2-3 - Like newborn infants, long for the pure spiritual milk, that by it you may grow up into salvation—if indeed you have tasted that the Lord is good.

  His plans for you are always ones of FAVOR and BLESSING. Peace is His promise to those who trust in Him. Delight yourself in His goodness!

1. What is the Goodness of God and what does it mean to you personally?

2. Journal any God revelations today as you contemplate the above.

Day 4

Psalm 34:8 - Oh, taste and see that the Lord is good! Blessed is the man who takes refuge in him!

Isaiah 55:1 - "Come, everyone who thirsts, come to the waters; and he who has no money, come, buy and eat! Come, buy wine and milk without money and without price!

1. How can you make a choice today to become one who "digs in" to the goodness of our Lord?

2. List some ways to practically apply that choice.

Day 5

Jeremiah 31:12 - They shall come and sing aloud on the height of Zion, and they shall be radiant over the goodness of the LORD, over the grain, the wine, and the oil, and over the young of the flock and the herd; their life shall be like a watered garden, and they shall languish no more.

Delight yourself in the presence of the Lord at all times because it is not only what will bring your life contentment but will infuse peace and refreshment into those you encounter in your life. Fullness of joy will change your life into one that will be like a well-watered garden.

1. How can embracing a lifestyle of delight in the presence of God bring you to a place of contentment?

2. Take time to rejoice in His goodness. Journal your thoughts.

Day 6

Re-read *"Summers Stirring of Our Senses – The Gift of Taste"*.

1. What changes have you felt in your spirit this week as you have adjusted "nibbling" thinking into "digging in" thinking?

2. Enjoy quiet time today sitting in the Presence of our King. Listen to His voice and allow a thankful heart to stir delight in His goodness and love for you.

You are His Beloved!

Summers Stirring of Our Senses
The Gift of Touch

The touch of contentment that we find in summer is as subtle as a breath of warm fresh air. It brings with it the warmth of sunrays and breezes that caress and cool. These touches wrap around us almost without our knowledge that they are present.

The touch of soft green grass on bare feet, a dive into a cool refreshing pool of water and a barefoot walk on a sandy shore are experiences of summer that we can again choose to enjoy or allow ourselves to pass up for lack of time or desire to experience them.

Summer brings an assortment of wonderful life filling experiences. The big decision often presents itself along with a personal question: "What do I give myself and time to in order to enjoy my summer this year?" We then chase after that which we have decided is the best fit.

The sense of touch is a very personal one to all of us. A physical touch signifies many things. It can be a touch of affection, one of encouragement, of greeting, or of joy. There are also many that bring pain – ones of rejection and anger – a push, a slap or a punch. Many of these – good and bad - we have experienced during our lives.

In a life that is filled with conflict and struggle our need for positive physical touch often causes us to look to others.

In our physical or emotional seeking for acceptance, affirmation and validation - physical touch pushes us into a "needy" place. This place pulls us away from the plans and purposes that Christ has for our lives. Our focus becomes similar to our deciding on what summer activities we want to enjoy. We are then looking and deciding according to what we think feels like a fit – or one of chasing after our needs - not one that is content in who we are in Christ.

His touch is what we truly crave for complete understanding of who we are in Him. All of our acceptance, affirmation and validation needs disappear as our focus is removed from US and placed on HIM.

The touch of the Holy Spirits presence has been given to you as a gift from Jesus and is a continual revelation of the Father's desire to walk among and with you in your life journey. This promise belongs to everyone who believes and it is His great delight to pour into you like a breeze that it is always available to cool and caress. His touch, His acceptance, His affirmation, His validation is ALL you need now and for eternity. His touch brings you to the feet of Jesus and brings your focus to being one that is all about the Lordship of Christ and bringing glory to Him.

Keeping your focus on the face of Jesus brings you complete freedom and contentment just as the warm fresh breeze that wraps around you in summer time.

Join me and bask in the touch of the Fathers hand, feel the caress of the Holy Spirits breeze and the intimate kiss of Lord Jesus.

Day 1

Spend some time contemplating what *"Summers Stirring of Our Senses – The Gift of Touch"* means to you.

1. What does this mean to you?

2. How does it apply to your life?

Day 2

Matthew 11:28-30 - Come to me, all who labor and are heavy laden, and I will give you rest. Take my yoke upon you, and learn from me, for I am gentle and lowly in heart, and you will find rest for your souls. For my yoke is easy, and my burden is light."

Making a choice to lay down all of our need for approval and validation requires a place of contentment and peace at our core. That peace and contentment comes from faith and knowing that we are loved. With that knowledge freedom from living to please, to be better, to measure up, etc. will disappear. For our eyes will be focused on our Lord.

1. Have you found yourself in the TRYING mode...needing someone to approve or tell you how good you are? You are not alone, but let's decide today to take up His yoke not our own. What would that look like for you?

2. Where do you find areas of your life that could use a complete "self-focused" cleaning?

3. Take time with Jesus today and let Him take off those burdens.

Day 3

Isaiah 58:11 - And the LORD will guide you continually and satisfy your desire in scorched places and make your bones strong; and you shall be like a watered garden, like a spring of water, whose waters do not fail.

1 Timothy 6:6-8 - But godliness with contentment is great gain, for we brought nothing into the world, and we cannot take anything out of the world. But if we have food and clothing, with these we will be content.

1. Contentment comes from deep within. Focusing on Him and not our own needs will foster that type of spirit. Jot down areas of your life you are content in and areas you struggle with.

2. Take time today to sit in His presence, lay down all of these and delight in who He has created you to be.

Day 4

Romans 15:13 - May the God of hope fill you with all joy and peace in believing, so that by the power of the Holy Spirit you may abound in hope.

Psalm 16:11 - You make known to me the path of life; in your presence there is fullness of joy; at your right hand are pleasures forevermore.

Knowing the gentle touch of the Holy Spirits breath upon you will bring freedom and contentment as you yield and listen. Decisions made while sitting and listening to the intimate voice of the Holy Spirit will direct you to the places that Christ has destined for your life.

1. What current decisions do you need a little help or direction with?

2. Write down your own pros and cons that come with those decisions.

3. Take time to bring those to the feet of the Lord and listen to His plans. (This may take you several "God time visits" to complete) Now re-adjust your plans to His plans.

4. Journal your experience.

Day 5

Psalm 42:7-8 - Deep calls to deep at the roar of your waterfalls; all your breakers and your waves have gone over me. By day the LORD commands his steadfast love, and at night his song is with me, a prayer to the God of my life.

Zephaniah 3:7 - The LORD your God is in your midst, a mighty one who will save; he will rejoice over you with gladness; he will quiet you by his love; he will exult over you with loud singing.

The goodness and love of the Lord is the only touch that brings complete contentment. Keep your focus on His face and peace will reign in your life.

1. Take time today to rejoice and delight in whom it is that holds you in the palm of His hand. Journal your thoughts.

Day 6

Re-read *"Summers Stirring of Our Senses – The Gift of Touch"*.

1. What revelations have you received this week about laying down your needs for validation and approval of man in exchange for the His?

2. How does understanding who you are in Christ change those needs and bring contentment?

You are created in His image!

Summers Stirring of Our Senses
The Gift of Smell

Smell is one of our senses that can trigger more memories in our lives than any others. Summers plethora of smells range from sweet flowers, fresh cut grass, grilling meat, burning campfires and salty waters to wet dogs and rotting vegetables.

How we respond to a scent will program it into our memories. Sweet flowers and fresh cut grass are distinct aromas – to the allergy sufferer they are to be avoided – to others enjoyed. The same goes for all smells – except maybe the rotting vegetables – which should be avoided at all costs.

In the spiritual, our very presence to those around us has an aroma. It can draw people to us or chase them away.

Is your smell one of enjoyment or one of rot?

Your life in Christ can be one that is like Mary who desired the ONE THING – to sit at the feet of Jesus or one like Martha that is busy about the "to do's" and represents judgment and law to those who don't believe. The scent that is expelled from you to those around you is an aroma of life or death.

Your love for Christ and those around you is a scent that is irresistible. Keeping your eyes on the face of Jesus will cause a contagious love to bubble out of your heart and along with that will be the expression of a scent of life.

Chose today to sit at the feet of Jesus. Focus on His face, allowing your love and contentment to rise to a level that only His love can accomplish in your life. His love will permeate your life and overflow to those around you. Your aroma will be one of love that will ignite memories of joy and love in the very atmosphere you live in - drawing others to find out what makes you smile. Then your joy will be made complete as you express His life and love to others.

Join me as we find contentment and delight in His presence. His aroma is the only scent my heart cries out for to carry within my being.

Day 1

Spend some time contemplating what *"Summers Stirring of Our Senses – The Gift of Smell"* means to you.

1. What does this mean to you?

2. How does it apply to your life?

Day 2

Proverbs 18:21 - Death and life are in the power of the tongue, and those who love it will eat its fruits.

Philippians 4:8 – Finally, brothers, whatever is true, whatever is honorable, whatever is just, whatever is pure, whatever is lovely, whatever is commendable, if there is any excellence, if there is anything worthy of praise, think about these things.

Our tongues are usually the source of "rot" that comes from inside of us. The things we think on daily are what fuel and fill us. These are often spewed forth as rot from our mouths.

1. Allow the above two scriptures to speak to your heart. Is your tongue being used to spread life or death to those around you?

2. Where do you see that you could change the "input" into your mind?

3. Take a few minutes and jot down a few things that are true, honorable, just, pure, lovely, commendable, excellent and worthy of praise to reflect on.

<u>Day 3</u>

John 14:6-7 - Jesus said to him, "I am the way, and the truth, and the life. No one comes to the Father except through me. If you had known me, you would have known my Father also. From now on you do know him and have seen him."

Colossians 3:15 - And let the peace of Christ rule in your hearts, to which indeed you were called in one body. And be thankful.

Proverbs 17:22 - A joyful heart is good medicine, but a crushed spirit dries up the bones.

Knowing that only Jesus brings forgiveness, peace and change will allow us freedom to lay down old ways and step forward into places where we can flourish and emit new life transforming contagious love.

1. A joyful heart is good medicine! Take time today to write down 10 things that bring joy to you.

2. Spend time in the Lords presence today rejoicing.

<u>Day 4</u>

Ephesians 2:8-10 - For by grace you have been saved through faith. And this is not your own doing; it is the gift of God, not a result of works, so that no one may boast. For we are his workmanship, created in Christ Jesus for good works, which God prepared beforehand, that we should walk in them.

Galatians 5:22-23 - But the fruit of the Spirit is love, joy, peace, patience, kindness, goodness, faithfulness, gentleness, self-control; against such things there is no law.

There are no works we can do to earn his forgiveness and make us righteous; that was already done for us at the cross as a free gift. The gift of the Holy Spirit is also just that – a gift. With His presence comes fruit that grows – changing us and allowing a new flavor to become desirous to those around us. Focused time at the feet of our Lord and the presence of the Holy Spirit will change us.

Our desire to be an aroma of life to those we daily come in contact with will draw us to the feet of Jesus and produce contagious fruit of the Spirit.

1. How do these two scriptures pertain to your life? Journal your thoughts as you consider each of them.

2. Spend time waiting in stillness today as you sit at His feet. Delight yourself in His presence.

Day 5

II Corinthians 2:15-17 - For we are the aroma of Christ to God among those who are being saved and among those who are perishing, to one a fragrance from death to death, to the other a fragrance from life to life. Who is sufficient for these things? For we are not, like so many, peddlers of God's word, but as men of sincerity, as commissioned by God, in the sight of God we speak in Christ.

This is a big assignment given to us as the bride of Christ. We are not up to the task without knowing who we are in Him. Who is sufficient for these things? None! However, we go forth with His authority and gift of the Holy Spirit. Walking only where, when and how He directs; staying under His reign at all times will allow us the life giving aroma of Christ.

1. Contemplate this assignment today as you silently wait in His presence.

2. Journal your thoughts from your waiting time.

Day 6

Re-read *"Summers Stirring of Our Senses – The Gift of Smell"*.

Isaiah 52:7 - How beautiful upon the mountains are the feet of him who brings good news, who publishes peace, who brings good news of happiness, who publishes salvation, who says to Zion, "Your God reigns."

As the body of Christ – His Bride – our mouth should be one that speaks only love, our feet should be seen as beautiful, bringing peace and our lives should pour out streams that make glad those we come in contact with. Our aroma should bring life, joy and love to the very atmosphere around us. This aroma will bring transformation that will spring forth from a spirit of contentment in who we are as children of our Lord and Savior Jesus Christ.

1. Summarize the revelations you received this week as you spent time in the word and at His feet.

You are His Aroma!

Transformation Awaits
Just Jump!

As the heat of summer begins its sizzle around us we look to the water to find the refreshing balance that our lives need. The shores of rivers begin to team with all ages of individuals looking for a way to delight themselves in its refreshment. The very presence of the cool river changes the atmosphere – internally and externally.

Just to sit on the edge of the river brings a semblance of coolness as its spray and breeze waft across our skin. Even our eyes seem to relax as we gaze at its movement.

Those who find the greatest pleasure at the rivers presence are those who in utter abandonment just jump into its waiting arms. They are completely immersed in its cool wet saturation. The joy that they experience is obvious. They emerge refreshed and transformed.

A hot, cranky, tired person is changed in a splash to a refreshed, exhilarated and joy-filled one.

As our lives bring us to a place of "over heated", finding the refreshment of a spiritual transformation also can be easily found if we run to the source.

Our source of refreshment and completeness is found at the river. Jesus is our source – our river. He promises us His presence and with that the Holy Spirit is available to bring transformation and comfort.

Our choices are to sit on the side of the river and receive a light breeze or occasional splash or we too can just jump in – overwhelmed by delight.

My choice is to just jump!

Total abandonment – immersed over my head – plunged into the depths!

The result is always immerging transformed, exhilarated refreshed and filled with joy.

Join me – Let's just jump!

Day 1

Spend some time contemplating what *"Transformation Awaits – Just Jump!"* means to you.

1. What does this mean to you?

2. How does it apply to your life?

Day 2

Psalms 36:5-9 - Your steadfast love, O Lord, extends to the heavens, your faithfulness to the clouds. Your righteousness is like the mountains of God; your judgments are like the great deep; man and beast you save, O Lord. How precious is your steadfast love, O God! The children of mankind take refuge in the shadow of your wings. They feast on the abundance of your house, and you give them drink from the river of your delights. For with you is the fountain of life; in your light do we see light.

Finding refreshment and refuge are always found at the source of utter contentment. The only true deep inner place to find that is in the steadfast love of the Lord. He desires you to drink from the rivers of His delight. It only takes our willingness to accept that place of fulfillment.

1. How would you describe the place you find refreshment and refuge?

2. What does it mean to you to find delight in drinking from His river of delight?

Day 3

Psalm 90:14 – Satisfy us in the morning with your steadfast love, that we may rejoice and be glad all our days.

Lamentations 3:22-23 - The steadfast love of the Lord never ceases; his mercies never come to an end; they are new every morning; great is your faithfulness.

His promise of refreshment is one that is new every morning – every hour – every minute – as necessary. What an amazing expression of His love for us.

1. Spend 15 min. today in a waiting - **silent** posture before the Lord – focus on the promise of refreshment and Joy.

2. Journal your thoughts.

Day 4

Psalm 107:9 - For he satisfies the longing soul, and the hungry soul he fills with good things.

Jeremiah 31:25 – For I will satisfy the weary soul, and every languishing soul I will replenish.

II Corinthians 3:18 - And we all, with unveiled face, beholding the glory of the Lord, are being transformed into the same image from one degree of glory to another. For this comes from the Lord who is the spirit.

1. When you are "overheated" where do you go and what do you do?

2. Do you find relief that refreshes your soul or a surface fix for the immediate moment?

3. Spend time today allowing the source – our river in Christ - to refresh your soul.

Day 5

Isaiah 55:12 - "For you shall go out in joy and be led forth in peace; the mountains and the hills before you shall break forth into singing, and all the trees of the field shall clap their hands.

Rejoicing and delight come from a heart that is saturated and overwhelmed by the goodness of God. Transformation erupts as you see who He is and how good He is to you. Abandonment is a total release of who you are and with it comes an indescribable freedom.

1. Are you one to sit on the edge of the river or jump in?

2. Journal your thoughts about both.

Day 6

Re-read *"Transformation Awaits – Just Jump!"*

1. How have you experienced transformation, refreshment and joy this week as you learned to delight in the goodness and love of Christ?

You are a New Creation in Christ!

Hesitant, Confident or "Sold-Out" Jumper?

As I observe the rivers activity on a hot sunny day I can't help but smile as I watch people prepare to jump into the river.

The long wooden dock extending out over the river allows for many to line up and jump into the waiting cool depths.

Everyone is dressed and ready for water play but you find many different approaches to accomplish the planned activity.

There are those who are hesitant, those who appear confident and those who are enthusiastic – coming with total abandonment as they approach.

Each of these three groups has different ways to actually obtain the result. No discrimination of age or sex, each of them plans on getting into the waiting arms of the refreshing water but how they achieve it is totally individualized.

First – the hesitant ones. They all look down and evaluate the water below; but then this group seems to find different ways to reach the goal. Sit and slide over the edge, stoop down and with a slight jump - land with a splash. Lastly those who seem somewhat braver - get right to the edge and jump straight off submerging with a slight cutting splash.

Now – the confident appearing ones. They also stop and look at the water below them but with less concern. They have decided that they are getting in and there is a very slight hesitation. But here too you find different jumping techniques. This group usually backs up and makes a running jump – some feet first, some "cannon ball" style, some with a bended knee dive. This group always reaches the water with a thunderous splash and is very aware that others are watching.

Then come the utterly "sold out" enthusiastic jumpers. This group knows the water is there and waiting so there is no need to step to the edge and look down. They don't notice or care about any on-lookers and they seem to jump according to some automatic instinct. They still have different styles of jumping – those who run and jump, those who "cannon ball, those who "belly flop" and those who cut the water with a deep knee dive. However, their goal is only focused on getting into the river and enjoying all the delight and refreshment it has to offer.

We will find ourselves in one of these three groups. As we compare these groups of jumpers to our own spiritual desire for all the delightful refreshment that is available to us through Christ, our style will become evident. These groups and each jumper's style will change over our spiritual lives.

Trusting Jesus in every detail of our lives will ultimately bring us to a place where we no longer need to look down to see if He - the water - is there.

We will know we are safe and the concern to be noticed as we jump will no longer direct our lives.

We will come with total abandonment and jump into the very presence of Jesus with trust in His complete fullness for our life.

How we jump differs – we are all different in our style of enjoyment of His presence – let go and just jump!

Trusting Him with all the details of your life leads to a life of full surrender. It will bring a contentment that will allow you freedom to walk into the center of the river and all that He has planned for your life.

Keep jumping until your depth of trust brings you to the center of His presence and the greatest depths and refreshment in Christ – total Lordship.

Day 1

Spend some time contemplating what *"Hesitant, Confident or "Sold-Out" Jumper?"* means to you.

1. What does this mean to you?

2. Which type of jumper do you see yourself as at this time in your life?

3. How does it apply to your life?

Day 2

John 15:7-9 - If you abide in me, and my words abide in you, ask whatever you wish, and it will be done for you. By this my Father is glorified, that you bear much fruit and so prove to be my disciples. As the Father has loved me, so have I loved you. Abide in my love.

John 8:31-32 - So Jesus said to the Jews who had believed him, "If you abide in my word, you are truly my disciples, and you will know the truth, and the truth will set you free."

Knowing that Christ always "has your back" is part of the trust process. Spending time both in His presence as well as His word strengthen that "knowing" within.

1. How does abiding in His presence and the bible deepen your trust?

2. Spend time today both in His presence and in the Bible reading.

3. Journal your thoughts from your time with Him today.

Day 3

Hebrews 11:1 - Now faith is the assurance of things hoped for, the conviction of things not seen.

Knowing the water is below you waiting to receive you as you jump requires an assurance of what is there. If you have to stop and look down then it becomes about your natural understanding. Faith in Christ grows from the "looking down" place to the "just jump" place once we know WITHOUT ANY DOUBT that HE loves us.

1. Describe your understanding of the love of Jesus for you personally.

2. Take time today to express your love for Him as you sit at His feet.

Day 4

Isaiah 12:2 - "Behold, God is my salvation; I will trust, and will not be afraid; for the Lord God is my strength and my song, and he has become my salvation."

Psalm 34:1 - I will bless the Lord at all times; his praise shall continually be in my mouth.

Psalm 118:24 - This is the day that the Lord has made; let us rejoice and be glad in it.

The "sold-out" jumper has no fear because the love of Christ has removed it. Trust has erupted into an enthusiastic desire to get close and delight in all the joy and refreshment that is waiting. An internal rejoicing shows in the face, the movement and the voice of those overwhelmed by His presence. Rejoicing in who He is begins that transformation.

1. We all have different styles in our times of rejoicing. What is your style and how do you express that before the Lord?

2. Take time again today to express new ways of rejoicing as you worship before Him.

Day 5

Psalm 150:1-6 - Praise the Lord! Praise God in his sanctuary; praise him in his mighty heavens! Praise him for his mighty deeds; praise him according to his excellent greatness! Praise him with trumpet sound; praise him with lute and harp! Praise him with tambourine and dance; praise him with strings and pipe! Praise him with sounding cymbals; praise him with loud clashing cymbals! Let everything that has breath praise the Lord! Praise the Lord!

Psalm 33:3 - Sing to him a new song; play skillfully on the strings, with loud shouts.

Psalm 37:4 - Delight yourself in the Lord; and he will give you the desires of your heart.

To live a life filled with delight is seen best through the eyes of a child. Fully content to be in the moment, no worry or concern and filled with joy. That is the desire of the Lord for His children.

1. How do you see yourself "Delighting in the Lord"?

2. What does it mean to you to live a life of contentment in Christ?

3. Spend time today contemplating these two questions as you wait and listen to the Holy Spirits stirrings within you. Journal His revelations to you and your thoughts.

Day 6

Re-read *"Hesitant, Confident or "Sold-Out" Jumper?"*.

1. As you have rejoiced through this week what changes have you seen and felt?

2. How can you implement a discipline of "trusting Him with the details of your life" and rejoicing in your life daily?

You are a child of the KING!

Float the Center of the River

The delight in summer's warmth brings us back to the comforting relief found in the cool waters of a tranquil river.

Along the banks are boisterous games being played, children running and laughing, barbeques crackling and emitting their inviting scents along with those whose feet and legs are engulfed in the refreshing dip of "just a little" water.

All of these activities bring joy and delight but looking to the center of the river you will find a lone rubber raft floating and rolling along with the current.

My desire draws me to that singular place. There in the center of the river the water is the deepest and most refreshing. There it flows with a pure clarity. In that place you find quietness; all activity on the rivers edge melts away and is silenced. The current in the center is in total control – freely flowing.

In Christ – our center of the river –we find the deepest water, purity and complete refreshment. There is peace and rest in that center as our control is given up and His face is our focus.

His love for us is deep and wide and He beckons for our presence to come and join Him. When we decide to step into the river our control is laid down. As we place our focus upon the source of our fulfillment – Jesus – then we are free to flow with the rivers current.

Our plans and purposes become nil as we allow the current to take us deeper into the center. Soon where the current goes we will find freedom as we float where it leads.

All thoughts of "our" plans float away. Delight in His presence brings clarity to our purpose. It is ALL about HIM. HE is our center and with that understanding comes a deep contentment to enjoy the float in the center of the river.

Join me in the safest, most refreshing river raft run of your life – one that is totally out of your control.

<u>Day 1</u>

Spend some time contemplating what *"Float the Center of the River"* means to you.

1. What does this mean to you?

2. How does it apply to your life?

Day 2

Isaiah 32:18 - My people will abide in a peaceful habitation, in secure dwellings, and in quiet resting places.

Psalm 51:6 - Behold, you delight in truth in the inward being, and you teach me wisdom in the secret heart.

His desire is for us to live in peaceful, restful – stress free places. Our desires dictate that place. He calls us to come away and sit with Him, we can chose to go to the center of the river or enjoy what He has given us on the riverbank. Both are good gifts; neither is wrong.

1. Where do you find yourself now – on the riverbank or desiring more of Him in the center of the river?

2. Are you happy and content in that place? If not, lets see how we can move into the center.

3. Spend time at His feet today – delighting in who He is.

Day 3

Galatians 2:20 - I have been crucified with Christ. It is no longer I who live, but Christ who lives in me. And the life I now live in the flesh I live by faith in the Son of God, who loved me and gave himself for me.

Moving into the center of the river – deeper water – is a place where our hearts cry "less of me – more of you" as we sit at the feet of Jesus. It means laying down control and trusting Him with the complete direction of our lives.

1. What areas of your life have you continued to hold onto and control - for fear of what the cost might be if you laid it down?

2. Take time today praying the above scripture as well as listening to His direction as you make choices about those areas of control.

Day 4

2 Corinthians 5:14-15 - For the love of Christ controls us, because we have concluded this: that one has died for all, therefore all have died; and he died for all, that those who live might no longer live for themselves but for him who for their sake died and was raised.

The love of Christ is what draws us into a place where our desires are transformed into His desires. With that comes the ability to lay down our own plans and trust in His plans and control. We begin a life filled with contentment. His plans and purposes for our lives are always far better than any that we could think or imagine. So letting ours go in place of His is a step that releases us into a journey that is filled with His glory.

1. What plans and dreams for your future do you have?

2. Spend time today sharing your thoughts about those plans with the Lord and listen to the confirmation or directions that the Holy Spirit may speak. Journal this time.

Day 5

John 7:37-39 - On the last day of the feast, the great day, Jesus stood up and cried out, "If anyone thirsts, let him come to me and drink. Whoever believes in me, as the Scripture has said, 'Out of his heart will flow rivers of living water.'" Now this he said about the Spirit, whom those who believed in him were to receive, for as yet the Spirit had not been given, because Jesus was not yet glorified.

As you step into the center of the river with Christ, the clarity of your life becomes all about HIM. Often He re-directs plans and dreams you have chased after for many years. Allowing your control to be given over to Christ brings with it a contentment and delight that far outweighs any of your plans. Peace will begin to reign in your life where stress and struggle previously had a tight hold. Focusing on HIM draws you to the center of the river and the current is in control. His plans then become clear and He will open doors and favor over you. You will then begin to step into the exact plans for your life that were designed for you to accomplish before you were born.

1. What does the above scripture say to you about desiring to step into the center of the river?

2. Does peace reign in your life? If not, what is the Holy Spirit saying to you regarding a key to finding that?

3. Spend time today at His feet moving into the center of the river with Him. Journal your thoughts regarding your time with Him.

<u>Day 6</u>

Re-read <u>*"Float the Center of the River"*</u>.

1. What revelations from scriptures, the prose writing, your personal time with God and your journaling have you received this week?

2. Summarize the impact these will make on your life.

You are Highly Favored!

We Are His Chosen Stones

As the sun begins to rise over the still surface of the lake, not a single ripple stirs. The quiet morning allows for the beckoning opportunity of skipping a stone across its glassy surface. The desire wins and the stones are carefully chosen.

As one stone after another is strategically thrown, a cascade of movement begins to shimmer. In ripples it begins its expansive advancement across the width of the lake. Each stone bounces several times before finding its final silent descent. The once still surface now coming alive with ripples in all directions reaching to the distant shore.

Watching the change that a few chosen stones can make draws my mind to contemplate our lives as those chosen stones – strategically cast upon His waters – our world, our country, our community, our family.

As chosen stones in our Lords hand we have been strategically released into the atmosphere that surrounds our daily lives.

As a stone resting in His hand we are ready to be released. We silently wait for the movement and ripple effect that our very presence will bring. That effect depends not on the stones presence but the pitchers determination and original intent. His desire is the catalyst.

Some skipping stones skip once, some twice and some multiple times – again determined only by the pitchers intent.

As our pitcher releases us - each in different directions the effect on the very atmosphere of our community will be as a ripple movement upon the lake. An expansive advancement will cascade outward pulling the broken, hurting and lost in its wake into the Kingdom of God.

Alone, one stone makes it's own impact but as each stone connects to the ripples of others our impact will change a still unmoving community into one filled with shimmering life - the gift of eternal life in Christ.

As a child of the King – let's allow our presence to bring a joyous ripple effect to those around us. For we are His chosen stones and are commissioned to bring the Kingdom of Heaven to those we encounter.

Day 1

Spend some time contemplating what *"We Are His Chosen Stones"* means to you.

 1. What does this mean to you?

 2. How does it apply to your life?

Day 2

Ezekiel 20:41 - As a pleasing aroma I will accept you, when I bring you out from the peoples and gather you out of the countries where you have been scattered. And I will manifest my holiness among you in the sight of the nations.

1 Peter 2:4-6 -As you come to him, a living stone rejected by men but in the sight of God chosen and precious, you yourselves like living stones are being built up as a spiritual house, to be a holy priesthood, to offer spiritual sacrifices acceptable to God through Jesus Christ. For it stands in Scripture:
"Behold, I am laying in Zion a stone, a cornerstone chosen and precious, and whoever believes in him will not be put to shame."

The love of Christ is an aroma that permeates our lives. Sharing His free gift of grace and mercy will transform lives around us as we simply love and freely express our faith in our daily lives.
Living a life filled with the Delight of the Lord allows the aroma within you to contagiously explode.

1. Do others around you know that you are a follower of Christ? Do you speak freely and openly of your faith?

2. Spend time today at the feet of Jesus and contemplate your answers above. Journal your thoughts.

Day 3

1 Peter 2:9-10 - But you are a chosen race, a royal priesthood, a holy nation, a people for his own possession, that you may proclaim the excellencies of him who called you out of darkness into his marvelous light. Once you were not a people, but now you are God's people; once you had not received mercy, but now you have received mercy.

2 Corinthians 4:6 - For God, who said, "Let light shine out of darkness," has shone in our hearts to give the light of the knowledge of the glory of God in the face of Jesus Christ.

Matthew 28:18-19 – And Jesus came and said to them, "All authority in heaven and on earth has been given to me. Go therefore and make disciples of all nations, baptizing them in the name of the Father and of the Son and of the Holy Spirit,"

1. As a royal priesthood, a Bride of the King what power and authority do we have?

2. Meditate on what it means to carry His name as our name – and that ALL that belongs to Him belongs to us. Journal your thoughts.

Day 4

Romans 10:11-17 - For the Scripture says, "Everyone who believes in him will not be put to shame." For there is no distinction between Jew and Greek; for the same Lord is Lord of all, bestowing his riches on all who call on him. For "everyone who calls on the name of the Lord will be saved."
How then will they call on him in whom they have not believed? And how are they to believe in him of whom they have never heard? And how are they to hear without someone preaching? And how are they to preach unless they are sent? As it is written, "How beautiful are the feet of those who preach the good news!" But they have not all obeyed the gospel. For Isaiah says, "Lord, who has believed what he has heard from us?" So faith comes from hearing, and hearing through the word of Christ.

Matthew 5:14-16 - "You are the light of the world. A city set on a hill cannot be hidden. Nor do people light a lamp and put it under a basket, but on a stand, and it gives light to all in the house. In the same way, let your light shine before others, so that they may see your good works and give glory to your Father who is in heaven.

1. How do these two scriptures relate to you being a stone that the Lord has tossed out onto the waters?

2. Journal your thoughts about applying them.

Day 5

Isaiah 61: 1-11 - The Spirit of the Lord God is upon me, because the Lord has anointed me to bring good news to the poor; he has sent me to bind up the brokenhearted, to proclaim liberty to the captives,
and the opening of the prison to those who are bound; to proclaim the year of the Lord's favor, and the day of vengeance of our God; to comfort all who mourn; to grant to those who mourn in Zion—
to give them a beautiful headdress instead of ashes, the oil of gladness instead of mourning, the garment of praise instead of a faint spirit; that they may be called oaks of righteousness, the planting of the Lord, that he may be glorified. They shall build up the ancient ruins; they shall raise up the former devastations; they shall repair the ruined cities, the devastations of many generations. Strangers shall stand and tend your flocks; foreigners shall be your plowmen and vinedressers; but you shall be called the priests of the Lord; they shall speak of you as the ministers of our God; you shall eat the wealth of the nations, and in their glory you shall boast.
Instead of your shame there shall be a double portion; instead of dishonor they shall rejoice in their lot; therefore in their land they shall possess a double portion; they shall have everlasting joy.
For I the Lord love justice; I hate robbery and wrong;

I will faithfully give them their recompense, and I will make an everlasting covenant with them. Their offspring shall be known among the nations, and their descendants in the midst of the peoples; all who see them shall acknowledge them, that they are an offspring the Lord has blessed. I will greatly rejoice in the Lord; my soul shall exult in my God, for he has clothed me with the garments of salvation; he has covered me with the robe of righteousness, as a bridegroom decks himself like a priest with a beautiful headdress, and as a bride adorns herself with her jewels. For as the earth brings forth its sprouts, and as a garden causes what is sown in it to sprout up, so the Lord God will cause righteousness and praise to sprout up before all the nations.

1. The realization of the authority that we carry in the name of Jesus Christ is one that can transform our lives and the atmosphere we live in if we step into that authority. In the above scripture – What parts "jumped" into your spirit as you read them? Is this an area that the Holy Spirit may be calling you to step into?

2. Spend time at the feet of Jesus today and journal any specific directions or thoughts He may stir.

Day 6

Re-read *"We Are His Chosen Stones"*.

1. Summarize your thoughts about this weeks prose.

2. During the last 3 months how is your life being re-directed to a place of Delighting yourself in the Lord?

You are His Beloved!

<u>Notes</u>

<u>Notes</u>

Titles available by J.K. Sanchez

<u>Majestic Reflection Devotional Study Series:</u>

Winters Rest

Spring's Assurance

Summer's Delight

Fall's Yield

<u>Stand alone or companion journals:</u>

Winters Rest Journal

Spring's Assurance Journal

Summer's Delight Journal

Fall's Yield Journal

Majestic Reflection Journal

Reflections of His Glory Journal

<u>Additional Titles</u>

Reflections of His Glory

Contact me at: <u>Judy@jksanchez.com</u>

Jksanchez.com

Also find me on Amazon.com

About the Author

J. K. Sanchez has lived and raised her three children in the Pacific Northwest where she and her husband of 40 years live and enjoy its beauty. As a writer and photographer her love of nature has flourished and is portrayed both through visually descriptive prose as well as through the eye of the camera.

Having ministered in many areas of the body of Christ her love for people and passion for worship and the presence of the Lord continually draw her to see freedom proclaimed and released to others through the finished work on the cross of Jesus.

www.ingramcontent.com/pod-product-compliance
Lightning Source LLC
Chambersburg PA
CBHW060308050426
42448CB00009B/1759